CW00493598

Commissioned by Ovalhoı
from The Basement, Cambridge Jui
under East.By.South.East. Fundc

THIS IS HOW WE DIE

Christopher Brett Bailey

was premiered at Norfolk and Norwich Festival, 15th May 2014

Written and Performed by Christopher Brett Bailey

Dramaturg: Anne Rieger

Musicians: George Percy, Alicia Jane Turner,
Nick 'Apollo' DeBenito Gellner, Christopher Brett Bailey

Lighting Design by Sherry Coenen

Produced by Beckie Darlington

Cover Art by Julian Martinez Milla

Photo by Matthew Humphreys

Christopher Brett Bailey

Christopher is a maker and writer of theatre, author of the award-winning punk-opera *The Inconsiderate Aberrations of Billy the Kid* and an Associate Artist of theatre/performance company Made In China. As a performer he has appeared at National Theatre, BBC, BAC, Almeida and in the bowels of the Top Secret Nuclear Bunker at Kelvedon Hatch. He is also a composer and performer of music and sound – the electronic 1/2 of ambient music duo Moon Ate the Dark and leader of guitar-noise project *THIS MACHINE WON'T KILL FASCISTS BUT IT MIGHT GET YOU LAID.* His performance training came from East 15 Acting School's Contemporary Theatre degree and he later attended Goldsmiths College, University of London where he earned an MA in Writing for Performance. This is his first published work. www.christopherbrettbailey.com

THANKYOUS (frm the bttm of my hrt):
benoit charland, carly davis, jess latowicki, tim cowbury,
andy field, ira brand, debbie pearson, rebecca atkinson lord,
faith dodkins, daniel pitt, pasco q kevlin, helen medland,
tim harrison, abby butcher, liz moreton, kevin wratten, leah
burdon manley, steve wood, joy martin, sammy metcalfe,
mom, dad and most of all: the 8 collaborators credited here.
i love you sisters & brothers!

CRITICAL ACCLAIM FOR THIS IS HOW WE DIE

WINNER: Arches Brick Award at Edinburgh Festival 2014

WINNER: Off West End Theatre Award in the category TBC Award (for productions that defy traditional categories) 2015

'an absurd road movie of the soul cut with a razor wit and bubbling paranoia.' Lyn Gardner, *The Guardian* ★★★★

'blisteringly brilliant. a staggeringly eloquent piece of work.' *The Scotsman* ★★★★

'a mirror for something rotten deep down in the centre of things...blasts the hypocrisies of contemporary culture.' *Exeunt* ★★★★★

'a glorious piece of work and about as good as Fringe theatre gets.' *Female Arts* ★★★★★

'electrifyingly good' *Everything Theatre* ★★★★

'He delivers the audience to some sort of higher providence... This is not merely a must-see, but a theatrical rite of passage' *A Younger Theatre*

'a visceral, world-burning piece...a brutal, vital, incredible show.' *Total Theatre*

'dirty and bloody and totally fucking exhilarating... Theatre you feel in your gut and on your skin.' Catherine Love

'My God. MY GOD.' *Synonyms for Churlish*

'Is this actually how we die? Driven at disorientingly high speed through the blazing landscape of our own riot-torn hearts, while the radio blares adverts for impossible products conceived in the agonizing heat of capitalism's terminal inferno? Christopher Brett Bailey auctions off everything we have and everything we think we know to the lowest bidder, leaving us stripped and spent and blissed out and beaten by language, that treacherous stuff we had thought was our friend. No, there ain't no sanity clause: but I'd trust Bailey with my life, and if this is how we die, you know, it's really not such a bad way to go.'
Chris Goode

'an annihilation of the senses' *Time Out (London)* ★★★★

'transfixing...a glorious pedal-to-the-metal trip that will leave you grinning and panting and maybe panicking, and gurning for more.' *Time Out (Sydney)* ★★★★

'a dark, venting, ragingly brilliant piece of theatre... sit down, strap in, shut up and listen.' *TV Bomb* ★★★★★

'utterly absorbing, a powerful performance that you not only lend your eyes and ears to but, by the end, that you lend your soul to.' *Literature Without Borders* ★★★★★

'what a fucking genius' *Smiths Magazine*

'THIS IS HOW WE DIE is the perfect treat for those experimental, left-field types who revel in questioning the nature of existence, but for those not interested, this is pretentious surrealist tosh.' *British Theatre Guide*

First published in 2014 by Oberon Books Ltd
521 Caledonian Road, London N7 9RH
Tel: +44 (0) 20 7607 3637 / Fax: +44 (0) 20 7607 3629
e-mail: info@oberonbooks.com
www.oberonbooks.com

Copyright © Christopher Brett Bailey, 2014

Reprinted in 2015, with revisions in 2017

Christopher Brett Bailey is hereby identified as author of this
play in accordance with section 77 of the Copyright, Designs and
Patents Act 1988. The author has asserted his moral rights.

All rights whatsoever in this play are strictly reserved and
application for performance etc. should be made before
commencement of rehearsal to the author c/o Oberon Books Ltd.
No performance may be given unless a licence has been obtained,
and no alterations may be made in the title or the text of the play
without the author's prior written consent.

You may not copy, store, distribute, transmit, reproduce or
otherwise make available this publication (or any part of it) in
any form, or binding or by any means (print, electronic, digital,
optical, mechanical, photocopying, recording or otherwise),
without the prior written permission of the publisher. Any person
who does any unauthorized act in relation to this publication may
be liable to criminal prosecution and civil claims for damages.

A catalogue record for this book is available from the British
Library.

PB ISBN: 9781783191970
E ISBN: 9781783196968

Cover design by Julian Martinez Milla

Printed and bound by 4edge Limited, Essex, UK.
eBook conversion by CPI Group (UK) Ltd, Croydon, CR0 4YY.

Visit www.oberonbooks.com to read more about all our books
and to buy them. You will also find features, author interviews and
news of any author events, and you can sign up for e-newsletters
so that you're always first to hear about our new releases.

manhood is measured in pussies per mile, how many pussies to the gallon. how many women have you fingered, have you fucked? but it seems to me the manliest a man can be is to be the man that gets fucked by other men. it is better to give than to receive. that's enough of your jail-cell logic, pussyfart. we're both inside and you're inside me. all the great fashions came from inside a prison. tattoos, baggy trousers, low-slung homosexuality – all started inside a prison. and if a man beats a woman he's a coward and if a man beats a man he is a hero, a neanderthal maybe, but a hero for sure.

we are killing ourselves and we have approximated hell. a generation of forever-babies bathing in radio waves and rocket fuel. under satellite and sedation, where did our paranoia go?

we live in a time of one gender, one race, one homogenous, milky, all-tolerant whole. me and you kid, we're exactly the same on account of being here in shared space and shared time. any difference you perceive is programming that must be eradicated, a cancerous rogue-thought laying tracks across your brain that will be unpicked by government needle. pincers enter for a key-hole surgery through fresh lips sliced into the top of your head, tracing errant thought threads to their source impulses and unpicking them 100 thoughts per second, clusters of unauthorised impulses and seed ideas knotted like chinese takeout on chopstick, fed back through the lips in your head and examined under electric light. careful those thought threads aren't long enough to wrap round your

neck and hang you with cause i wouldn't put it
past them.

and the obituary reads: a young man, a young
woman, hey what's the difference, died today
during a government-subsidized emergency
mandatory surgery to the brain, coroner says
there may've been pain and officials say if there
was they probably deserved it. also dead today
are the olsen twins, following shotgun blasts
to their collective identity. cut this coupon out
and get 1/3 off your next visit to our digital
marketplace. you can buy fishguts and stolen
radios without even getting off the victoria line.
isn't progress a wonderful thing? our age and
the age before ours trips over itself, farting out
cliches and the freshest one is self-reflexive, the
freshest one is this: political correctness has gone
mad. gone mad. and i ask for a definition of mad
and i am lead to understand that this cliche itself,
with its casual use of the word mad, proves there
is yet more linguistic whitewashing to be done
if the perceived goal is to be the achieved goal.
and i ask you, who is this straightjacket built
for? have you heard our fresh cliche uttered by
anyone of colour or minority persuasion? or is
it the kneejerk chant of the great white alone?
i have never met a black man who did not call
himself a nigger, a rentboy who was not proud
to be a whore. these are letters, words, sounds
made with the mouth, they are meaningless,
they are weapons of our own construction, of
a mutual agreement based on idiocy, they are
weapons of the past, they are only weapons if
you treat them as such and can be dismantled
any time, any place. they carry no more
meaning than god, love, fate or any other magic

carpet lithium crutch deployed by the weak to
carry them through the desert and get them
through dinner conversation. clinking glasses,
fizzy wine flows and suddenly he doesn't look
quite so equine. daddy always loved them jewish
comedians but wouldn't he shit out a jackboot
if ya brought one home? and wouldn't that be
exciting? the look on his face at breakfast. jews
eat bacon don't they? this is the 21st century. or
is everyone a vegetarian now? last train soon
and i can't remember if i'm wearing matching
underwear. fuck it, he can't be that shallow. he's
a jew. they are smarter than us aren't they? now
did they invent humour or did they just slap
a trademark on it? slick tom breathes nicotine
and tar deep into his lungs back when that was
okay to do in the workplace, blue smoke curling
round his brown ringlets, the last seconds of
a jethro tull climax spinning on a record deck
transmitting to truck cabs and taverns on both
sides of the river. leaning into the microphone,
going once more to the phones and this time
it's a woman who wants to hear that one by
blue oyster cult and he tells her that she's a wet
dream and that he'll gladly play her song. the
needle drops and i'm pressed up against the
window of the control booth, staring in from the
street, barely tall enough to reach the window,
snow melting in my size fours, and i'm in love
because i too like that one by blue oyster cult. in
love with her, with him, with the whole situation
and the next year they move the station out
to the suburbs where the rent is lower and the
transmission signal is stronger. you can find the
station online these days. but it's just not the
same.

they gave him a desk for the day but he was a
writer of nightmares, couldn't write in the day.
took a stab at a daymare and ended up with a
book about horses. surprise surprise it didn't sell.

keep up junior, we're Evolving and the odds of
you winning the thumb war aren't looking good.

in our city black and white segregation no longer
exists as it once did, it is no longer black, it is no
longer white, except in extreme circumstances
and extreme minority and any white person
that has lived in one of our few black
neighbourhoods will tell you: it's the other white
people you are crossing the street to avoid. these
hulking vermin, frothing idiocy at the mouth,
pooling in their palms. an army of pram pushing
proud parents pushing sacks of undead white
meat towards forever. intelligent woman a turns
to intelligent woman b and says 'who would
dare to bring a child into a world like this?' any
opinion you have you do not have absolutely,
that is, it is not 100% your opinion, or else you
are closing doors and rest assured something
valid has been overlooked. we sit in this room
looking at eachother, me from my seat, you
from yours, and the assumption is that we are
not enemies. the context implies that we are on
the same side. i am not concealing any weapons
and i trust that you aren't either. this bulge in my
pocket is not a revolver and if it is i will not be
using it to gun down my least favourite audience
member on the basis of first impressions. but
what if a disagreement should occur? what if

you heckle and with words as my only weapons
what if i am driven to pretending your death in a
manner most humiliating for the entertainment
of the audience seated around you. if, in our
collective fantasy, you are skinned alive or
melted from the inside then to what extent has
this actually happened? is it as real as any fiction
we share and if so, who do the wounds belong
to and where is the afterparty? champagne
bounces off the bottom of a glass and our hero is
telling us a story. the story of a party, where he,
the hero shook hands face to face with george
w bush. a simple adlib from me: 'fuck george w
bush' would set this room alight with whoops,
cheers and noises of general agreement because
we are glued to one another. remember: the
context implies that we are not enemies and this
bulge is not a revolver. together, we suffered and
blushed our way through 8 years of tyranny so
that christ could rise from the smouldering ashes
but wake up kiddies, christ aint nothing but the
old model with a new paint job. you fear and
you revere fictions, actors hired to play parts in
movies with infinite budgets, available on any
screen anytime and anywhere. champagne still
flows and our hero is approaching the punchline
wherein he stares georgey baby directly in the
eyes and asks how it feels to no longer be the
president. baby bush booms 'i was sick of being
fucked in the ass, junior: the end could not
come soon enough'. and just as roger moore
admits he was doing it for the money, here is
something we can all agree on. 'the end could
not come soon enough' and this bulge is still
not a revolver. the neurological effects of coffee
are thought to mirror that of cocaine but i don't
recommend you rub coffee into your partner's

genitals to prolong sexual intercourse. changing
trains from the northern to the central i see a
man in a sweater bearing the letters EDL – the
english defense league. i'm surprised, shocked,
pulse sprinting the 100 metre, the audacity of
this villain, this monster, this fool, to advertise
himself a villain, a monster, a fool in plainsight,
in public. just standing there, advertising hate
right on his shirt, and I slide into a fantasy
landscape parallel to our reality in which I shove
this man off the platform, onto the tracks and
his head is exploded into a cloud of dust by the
force of the oncoming train bearing down on the
track and the crowded platform cheers and in
that moment I slip out of the parallel and back
into our reality to find I am nursing a semi-
erect penis on a public train platform. the man,
stands peacefully, advertising the english defense
league and i, so thrilled by vivid conjurings
of his splintering skull and grey matter made
vapour, his demise, am advertising: nothing
but my own libido. the oncoming train pulls
peacefully into the station without crushing this
man's head and opens it doors to reveal a year
9 school trip and i wonder which one of us is at
this precise moment, spreading more hate.

she was waiting for me outside the school gates.

i had a backpack on.

we went to different schools.

she was leaning against the gate with a cigarette
hanging out of her mouse, dressed all in black.
no retro patterns. all black. and she never wore
black and she had a cigarette dangling out of
her mouse. she had a mouse where her mouth
should be. i didn't ask. but i did ask about the
black clothing. so i said 'what's with the black
clothing?' and she says 'i'm mourning the death
of our relationship'.

we dated for another 18 months.

'And in case you're wondering about the mouse'
she said 'i've decided to quit smoking. this
mouse is going to smoke for me.'

'is he like a pet?' i said.

'no, he's like an avatar. i wanna quit and this'll
make it easier cause i'll be able to continue
the ritual of smoking through him. and this
way we'll find out if smoking really is bad for
you. if the mouse dies we can safely assume
that smoking kills. if he doesn't die we'll know
that the surgeon general's warnings are hollow
propaganda.'

'that makes perfect sense.' i said.

gosh, she had a hell for a mind.

we arrived at her parents' place. and i had not
met them before. so i was nervous like. you

know. sweating in places I didn't even know I had sweat glands.

she had described her mother as the strong silent type

and her father as a walking swastika.

and i had assumed she was joking.

(she wasn't joking)

her mother was a body builder – bulging muscles, shaved head. into all that body modification stuff too; she had a row of staples holding her mouth shut.

…the strong and silent type.

and years before her dad had fallen out of a moving vehicle at top speed and broken every single bone in his body

he paid the doctors double to re-set all of his bones into the shape of a…

he was a neo-nazi, hitler used to visit him in his dreams…

we arrived at this little english cottage with a thatched roof. the kind that's on one of those narrow laneways that goes from nowhere to nowhere lined with hedges all the way. where the road is so narrow there's no pavement or shoulder, it's just road, road, road, road...wall of the house.

and were walking up to the place and i go 'man that'd keep me awake – i wouldn't wanna listen to the traffic' and she explains that her dad hasn't been able to drive since his accident and that he likes the noise of the cars.

especially the volkswagens.

her mom is so happy we've arrived that she whips the front door open with such force it breaks away from its hinges and she's left just holding the door as she waves us inside. we enter through the broken door and we go into the den and there's her dad...

dude's just a mess of right angles,

the man could barely sit down. and –

she'd previously described him as a walking swastika and that proved somewhat inaccurate. he couldn't walk – more sorta rolled. sorta threw himself forward and tumbled. sorta cart-wheeled. used to cart-wheel around the room – 65 years old, quite a spectacle.

so he rolls on over to us and parks up in front of me and i'm thinking it's a good thing he's not jewish – not least cause he'd hate himself, but he woulda needed six limbs to do an accurate star of david!

so he's parked up in front of me and he says it's
nice to meet me and i don't know which one of
his hands to shake cause he's got one arm that's
sorta dangling above his head and one that's
folded in on itself, sorta tickling his belly. so i opt
for that sorta half wave thing and that's when i
knew we were off on the wrong foot.

the four of us waste no time, we sit right down
for dinner. i'm sitting on one side of the table,
to my left she's there with her beehive looking
immaculate – and her mouse is on the table
stubbing a cigarette out on the side of her plate
– and i look at her and i think 'strong and silent
for a mom, walking swastika for a dad. god you
are so…literal. i love that.' and that's when i
think i *knew* i loved her. i mean that's always
when you know, isn't it? you meet the parents,
the family, and if you can put up with them and
your judgments of them don't reflect back in a
corrosive manner on the one that you're with…
then it might be love.

so, i'm sitting across from this human swastika
who can't even reach his mouth, he's sorta
leaning over and picking food off his plate
and just sorta dropping food into his mouth.
vegetables bouncing off his chin. and next to
him is this placid mountain of a woman. very
patiently taking staples out of her lips so she can
eat. veins bulging in her neck as she dines on
her body-builder's dinner – scooping dry whey
powder straight outta the bucket and sucking

raw eggs out of a chicken's ass. and i'm thinking
if i can put up with this…it must be love!

and that's when the conversation starts. my
beautiful heart-shaped bubble is burst by the
old-man's questioning:

'so my daughter tells me you're circumcised'

'well yeah, i mean if you're born in north
america in the 1980s it was pretty common
medical…'

'you're from jew york city, are ya?'

'well no actually i'm – '

'do ya drive? get yourself a volkswagen – '

'don't actually have my – '

'how do you feel about ozzie?' he says

now here finally a question i can answer: 'i like
the first couple sabbath records but after that…'

'no!' he screams and he smashes his dangling
hand down on the table splintering the ceramic
plate, food flies everywhere, the chicken
squawks and ducks for cover behind one of
strong-silent's gargantuan hands.

'oswald mosley you imbecile'

and this wave of tension just rolls through the
room.

both the ladies are completely silent.

the mouse is chain-smoking because of the
stress. and i realize that i have to step up to
the plate and i have to say something to this
monster.

...

i thought long and hard,

probably a bit too long and hard

and i said 'if i fell out of a moving vehicle and
broke all my bones i'd get them re-set to spell
"fuck you you fucking piece of nazi shit fuck
fuck"'

and then i turned to her and i said 'come on
babe, we're outta here.' and just at that precise
moment the wall broke open behind them and
the front end of a car came screaming into the
dining room, the tire ravaged the old man – his
limbs mangled in the tire well, the top half of
his head removed by the fender, the vinegar
juices of his evil cancerous brain spraying like
a geyser to the gods, the car has driven straight
into the dining room, disintegrating the old
man and travelling towards the old woman. a
headlight shatters on the rock-hard protrusion
of her cheekbone as the careening vehicle is
stopped dead by her iron bulk, the metallic
paneling of the car coccoons around her,
bending at the will of her indestructible body,
clearing the dinner table as it does so. we two
have to lean back to not get smacked in the face

with a passing rearview mirror. at the moment
of impact the passengers – a charming lesbian
couple who we now have a flatshare with – are
ejaculated through the windshield, broken
glass everywhere, their two bodies sent sailing
across the room and through the back wall of
the house, crash landing in the garden just a
steaming heap of broken bones, grass stains and
flannel shirts.

i look at her

she looks at me

and we agree: it's probably time to leave.

so the father's dead,

torn to pieces by the car

and the mother's peeling back the wreckage like
a steel artichoke to reveal…

that she's absolutely fine.

which i thought was a nice twist because except
for putting her mouth on a chicken's ass without
consent she hasn't really done anything wrong.

per se.

so we say 'thank you for the lovely meal' and i
do that fake yawn thing

and the strong/silent mother nods which i
assume means 'it's been great to meet you, travel
safe and stop by any time.'

so her and i get up from the table and the
mouse is hot-boxing the inside of the cigarette
packet and the three of us are approaching the
lesbian-shaped hole in the back wall of her
parents' house (and between the lesbian hole,
the car hole and the door off its hinges there's
no shortage of exit routes) and i glance back
to wink at the mother and i see that the father
is now leaking out across the linoleum and i
notice for the first time that the car bumper that
decapitated him? bears an Anti-Fascist League
bumper sticker. not only that. car's a fucking
volkswagen.

and i think 'god. it's the little things.'

we walk home cause neither one of us is in the
mood for an automobile ride and she's on her
mobile phone to one of her friends and she goes:

'nah. we've been to dinner with my parents.

didn't go well at all.

complete car crash'

and i think 'god. you are so literal…i love that.'

we shook our fists at the sky or at god or
maybe just at the satellites. and together we
imagined a river and we threw our cell phones
into it and the circuits sizzled in our made-up
water and our made-up current carried these
phones, these little tokens, these trinkets of our
times downstream and the metal bits suffered
discoloration and one phone sank to the bottom
and got a mouth full of sediment while the other
floated upstream through choppy water and
changing landscapes, perhaps it served as a boat
for some fishes that were tired of swimming or
perhaps it did not, but in any case it bobbed
and it glided. out of this hemisphere. out of
civilization. into arctic or antarctic waters. and
out of my fucking life. Its plastic shell shivering
as it navigates icebergs, its battery belching and
sputtering and i'd like to imagine dying a painful
and in any case permanent death far far out of
signal range, stranded, cold and unable to tell
its stupid fucking little friends that it's dying, it's
dying, it's dead.

and we shook our fists at the sky or at god or at
least at the satellites

'and when you say things like that…when you
use language like that'

she said.

'i just can't help but think maybe you're a
misogynist.'

uh no. i don't. that's stupid. firstly, i don't hate
women okay? i'm not a misogynist. and second
of all, secondly, two, B, whatever: you, you
hate all people. you're a misanthrope. and
mathematically? that's twice as bad!

why do we use isms to police each other? like
we are constantly trying to catch everybody
out around us – he's a racist or she's a zionist,
that's classist, or fascist, i'm a marxist in theory
but a reluctant capitalist in praxis, a modernist,
fundamentalist post-structuralist, right now i'm
a listist and i'm a little pist but you'd know it if
i was the pistist cause if i was the pististi'd be
begging you to fuckin' fist this.

a giant rubber cyst, emerging from the mist, do
you get my goddamn jist?

it's a list,

well done chris,

you've made a list. of things that end with ist.

but it's still just a list.

but the point is that those, that we're, that
we could maybe do without all that, why put
boundaries around what we think? it's not in
the interest of dialogue or empath- it's not very
humanist…! which is also an ist, so we gotta
take it off the list, not the ist list it is an ist so it
belongs on the list, gotta take it off the approved
list. …list is also an ist. so we <u>can't</u> have an
approved list… this is shit. this is shit. this is
hard. *(forehead in hands)*

and she thought about this for a long time.

long enough for me to take a nap, i walked to…
egypt in the time it took,

i went, i went around the world. the whole. and
it took more than 80 days let me tell ya, that
80 days shit's fucking false. advertising. i wasn't
even, i wasn't in a balloon. i was on foot. walked.
barefoot over…over broken glass. all the way
around the world. over broken glass. i mean,
there wasn't, it wasn't constant broken glass, ya
know, the path i was on didn't naturally intersect
THAT MUCH broken glass. but when it did i
was fucking diligent and i stepped on it, okay?

commitment. *(points at chest)*

i made it all the way around *(circle gesture)*

back to here

or there

or wherever

and she goes:

'i think maybe you should attack the ism, instead
of the ist. cause the ist is like...the person,
the individual: the chauvinist...the XXXist...
but you wanna destroy the concept, the over-
arching, ya know the enemy is up there, not
down here on our level, it's gotta be bigger than
us. you wanna destroy. so, i'd say attack the
ism...capitalism, feudalism, philanthropism and
that way when you attack it it's the concept that
dies, not the individual, not the person. and plus
there's a bunch of others that you miss out on if
you attack the ist. like vegetarianism. maybe you
wanna rail against vegetarianism but you can't
because vegetarianist? that aint a thing. so rail
against the ism. you should call it maybe: Death
to the Ism.'

i said

what about…

what about…

jissum?

jissum.

that's an ism.

jissum.

we both like that!

jissum.

jissum.

jissum.

that is. an ism.

jissum.

jissum.

jissum.

jissum.

i said it many many times and she didn't laugh
(either)

jissum.

jissum.

i basically spent the rest of my life saying it

jissum.

jissum.

jissum.

jissum.

ya know when?

jissum.

ya say a word so many times that it loses

jissum.

its meaning – becomes just sound –

jissum.

– just noise – – after a while

jissum.

jissum.

jissum.

jissum.

jissum.

jissum.

jissum.

jissum.

jissum.

jissum.

jissum.

jissum.

jissum.

jissum.

jissum.

jissum.

jissum.

jissum.

jissum.

jissum.

jissum.

jissum.

jissum.

jissum.

jissum.

jissum.

jissum.

jissum.

jissum.

jissum.

jissum.

jissum.

jissum.

jissum.

jissum.

jissum.

jissum.

jissum.

jissum.

jissum.

jissum.

jissum.

jissum.

jissum.

jissum.

jissum.

jissum.

jissum.

jissum.

jissum.

jissum.

jissum.

jissum.

jissum.

jissum.

jissum.

jissum.

jissum.

jissum.

jissum.

jissum.

jissum.

jissum.

jissum.

jissum.

jissum.

jissum.

jissum.

jissum.

jissum.

jissum.

jissum.

jissum.

jissum.

jissum.

jissum.

jissum.

jissum.

jissum.

jissum.

jissum.

jissum.

jissum.

36

jissum.

jissum.

jissum.

jissum.

jissum.

etc.

and she said:

        'chris.

                go fuck yourself.'

and i could tell she meant it, you know.

that she really wanted me to go.

…and to fuck myself.

so that's exactly what i did.

but i worked up to it, you know.

wanted to do it right.

with chivalry and romance. courtship.

and not in a gendered way, more sort of a quaint, retro kind of way.

so i texted myself.

ya know, started with something casual like 'heyyy (with three Ys). just saw this thing that reminded me of you and it's been aaages? drink soon?'

and then i had that butterfly thing in the pit of my stomach and i kept looking at my phone even though it hadn't made a noise and eventually i wrote myself a nice message back and even ended it with big X little x dot.

so, the half of me that was gonna play the boy went outside and stood on the front step of the house, all nervous like. rang my own doorbell.

i kept myself waiting, naturally.

eventually i came to the door in an outfit different from the one i was planning on wearing to dinner. i permitted myself to wait in the living room where i had just put some music on. something obscure that i thought would impress myself.

i went out to dinner and plied myself with wine and once or twice i stared into my own eyes for just a second too long.

there was a moment at the end of the evening when i wondered if i was coming on too strong.

so i checked in with myself and it turned out the feelings were mutual.

on the way upstairs to my place i held the door for myself which i hoped i would interpret as simple courtesy, not as a gendered act – afterall i was careful to not order on *my* behalf and i absolutely insisted that we split the cheque

(50-50)

i lead myself inside, i offered myself a glass of wine and i stood in front of the book case, awkwardly trying to block photographs of my ex, hoping that *i* wouldn't notice them. and kicking myself for not remembering to take them down before i invited myself up for a nightcap.

i was a tad nervous…which is pretty normal, first time with a new partner.

but i could tell i was nervous so i tried to give myself really clear and encouraging signals: i sat on the couch. i kept my body language very open. and i pretended not to notice when the back of my hand grazed my own thigh.

and as pleasant as it was i couldn't stop myself wishing i'd take some fucking initiative and just kiss myself already. it's not that the anecdote i was telling at the time wasn't amusing but it was getting late and one half of me had to be up early.

a few moments later i'm rolling around on the bed, desperately trying to unclasp my own brassiere. eventually i just batted my own hand away and took the goddamn thing off myself.

i tried to be attentive to my own needs throughout

and to not dictate the rhythm too much

there was a moment halfway through where both of us clearly wanted to be on top.

so i sacrificed my own needs and let *myself* finish on top.

and i'm proud to say that we had our orgasms at exactly the same time.

not bad for a first attempt with a new partner.

afterwards, half of me kinda wished it'd been a little more adventurous but the other half was glad to have saved a few 'moves' for next time.

and in the morning i was sure to tell myself that i was beautiful,

to walk myself down to my car

and to apologize for only having orange juice to offer myself for breakfast.

the minute i left i crawled back into bed and i'm not proud to tell you this but i texted my ex. i said: 'i did what you said, i called your bluff, i fucked myself and it was not very good. i just don't know if *i* click, ya know? and i don't look quite as good naked as i had hoped i would. and it could never become a real relationship

anyhow because i snore. and you know what i'm
like if i don't get my sleep. if you can forgive me
i want you back.'

together we imagined a river and we threw
our cell phones into it. and as water worked its
way into the cracks, corroding the insides and
destroying our little machines we had secret little
orgasms to celebrate the choices we had made.
and we said 'fuck you' to the sky, or to god, or
at least to satellites and anybody travelling in
international airspace. and we went directly to
the nearest bank and withdrew her inheritance
cheques. swastika man's life savings had come
through, and as the sky behind her head turned
blood orange which is just another shade of red
she whipped off her glasses to maximize impact
and she snarled 'let's hit the road, jack-off'. gah, i
thought: so. much. zeal.

squeezed it, ya know, like a tube of toothpaste?
emptied it of its muscle, its mucus, before,
without a clear passageway for oxygen to the
brain you are a) dead or b) as good as dead. and
the obituary reads. itself. cause it too knows the
rest of the paper is untrue. an injection of fear
in through the eyes, out through the actions,
in plain-speak jargon, tattooed onto this earth
and inked into forever. you got one choice. a
get-out clause. a chance to claw your way out.
the neurological effects of coffee are thought to
mirror that of cocaine and they both keep you
running back n forth to the bathroom. sun-baked
infinity in all directions, a savage thrust of white
noise and electronic sound, the sound of one
idea giving birth to another. a board room, a
boiler room, a graph of a pie chart of a projected
statistic sparkling or natural? sparkling gives

me a tummy ache. something to do with the
bubbles, no troubles. bubbles. racing through
this city's trademark standstill traffic, running
late, running on empty, not running at all, this is
century 21. plasterboard, billboard, a cartoon of
a memory of an advertisement for a song about
a movie you never saw but you feel like you did.
a melody on a harmony in a rhythm. between
us. not physically of course but in metaphor,
in memory, in ideal. as the bird flies or one
imagines the bird flies – a maze, a scattering,
everything equal, everything insignificant when
viewed from above. as the bird flies implies,
no – it means. it doesn't imply a goddamned
anything. as the bird flies means the shortest
distance between two points but who is to say
that birds would ever actually take the shortest
distance. if i was a bird i would fly in spaghetti
bowl patterns just to prove humans wrong, just
to contradict this arrogant hex of a species in my
own little greasy feathered, worm-chewing way.
and i'd fly high like marvin as high up as i could,
away from this gridlock of smart phones and
sandwich shops and i would tango dance across
the sky, i would glide on atmosphere's crest, i
would surf-sail on god's breath and i would get
sucked. straight into the propeller of a low-flying
747 in international airspace SPHFFF – my
body crinkled like christmas paper and shredded
like a quarterly water bill, would rain down
from this jet engine, from this 20th-century
innovation, from this bus of the air, it would rain
down towards earth or rather it would simply
fall in many pieces, it would fall at various
speeds in pieces of various size, it would not rain
as only water rains but it would fall like rain,
fuck it, it would rain. my little bird body would

rain down from the sky, sacrificed to metal and
scattered by the wind, chunks of would-be meat
that used to be me, sprinkled like tarragon or
cumin, yeah cumin, across this city – little flecks
of me raining down and landing on rooftops and
taxi cab windows, bouncing from umbrellas and
collecting like mist in your hair-do.

if i was a bird i'd be a vengeful badass but i am
not a bird.

tucked up by static and watched over by
satellites, we sleep, we rest

and occasionally, you and i,

we dream.

cocooned in a hum of pedal tones and distant
drones, like newborns. a conveyor belt – thinly
sliced rubber stretched between two rotating
cylinders – magic carpeting an object, a product,
you, your loved ones and your carry-on luggage,
straight into the circling storm, 'did you fuckin
see that, man? i said you fuckin see that?' i
don't much remember and i don't remember
much. fast asleep on the skin of a nightmare, our
children's children got a prepaid ticket directly
to the gates of (a pastel-coloured) heck. throwing
a brick through a window punishes the building
for ideas that it represents –

throw a brick at the person inside that building
instead –

gain access by disguising yourself as a UPS
delivery man with a small delivery of exactly
one brick, postmarked for the face of your
enemy. and ya know what? this package is
pay on delivery. price of postage? exactly one
broken fucking nose.

bathroom friend. friend for the night. cause who
knows what this bulge is but goddamn if that
powder aint white and as a great man once said:

THERE ARE NO GREAT MEN

yeah but if you'd listen…

a great man once said: 'there's nothing more/'

(hold on while i get the wording right)

'there's nothing more powerful than an idea
whose time has come'

what about all the ideas whose time has passed?

cause you and I live in a culture that doesn't just
kick its dead horses, it embalms them. It drags
them up in front of the class so the class can
worship them.

'there's no such thing as a new idea. everything
is stolen'

– bull.shit. –

there is no finite number of ideas: just. try.
harder. Anything that makes you feel bad for
trying is a roadblock to dissuade you from
fleeing this city as it burns to the fucking ground.

44

goddamnit we gotta get better ventilation in
here, 'did you fuckin see that, man? did you
fuckin see that?' sweat pours over fresh blisters
and the sun kisses the moon and they agree to
cross paths earlier tomorrow night to peruse the
handover notes in greater detail, and you and
I crawl, fat stomachs dragging through dirt and
into the woods, we are looking for a shady place
to die. cause it's dog eat dog and this dog has
had its day. to die with dignity. you and i. with
violin music. and a buffet tray. a shady place
to die. and once we're dead we'll need an even
nicer plot of land, an even shadier spot to dig a
hole and bury our bodies. cold concrete warmed
by electric cables. why do we store dead bodies?
electric current through steel wire, why DO we
store dead bodies?

why do we house dead people under our
ground?

cause you know there's no better use for land
than accommodating guests who have already
left the party.

it's real important that the deceased can stretch
their legs while they decompose.

cause if my tombstone wasn't a tombstone but
was a plaque on the mantel

or reck room wall

of a loved one

then that loved one would be forced to think
about me

once in a while.

If i die tonight, dear friends please, don't burn
my body or donate me to medical science. cause
i would prefer to be stored in the ground…
taking up just as much space as i did while i was
alive.

and i got a right to an opinion about this…even
after I'm dead.

but I promise to do my bit, ya know, provide a
service.

perhaps my skull could act as a refuge shelter for
germaphobic worms?

i am so glad there is no concrete proof that this
planet is struggling to support the people who
are still alive onnn ittt.

If we have to keep dead people around why
do we put them into the ground? This means
we can't grow anything in that ground, can't
build anything on that ground, can't pave over
that ground, can't even take a walk across that
ground, enjoying so-called nature, without being
reminded of other people's sadnesses.

death is not sad. losing people is sad. for you.
not for them. cause if you've lost somebody they
are either a) dead

or b) they wanted to be lost

by you.

unrequited love. that is sad. and i mean sad
in both senses: in the operatic, cosmic, crying
stone statues sense...and in the other sense too:
pathetic.

...

we killed a guy once.

on the the assumption that it was him or us.

retrospectively I'm not so sure it was him or us.

in fact, it's the one thing I feel bad about in all
of this.

you see our great big american road trip was
going so far so good.

a little too good maybe.

picture a gas station. one of those old-timey,
broken-down, two-fuel pump gas stations. and
we're in a desert or the dustbowl or whatever
– what matters is that it's flat and there's flies
landing on things you wish they wouldn't land
on. we've pulled into this gas station in our
rental car – not quite a cadillac but you can
picture a cadillac if that helps you. now, she's
driving cause i don't have a license, and she's
looking good – beehive hairdo, retro glasses,
the whole bit – and we're pulling into this
gas station to ask for directions, which to me
seems ludicrous cause as far as i can tell there's
only one long, straight road across this whole
goddamn state. So i get outta the car and i go
into the little hut, the little beat-up gas station
shack and just as i'm darkening the door of this
fine establishment with its broken wind chimes
and its shelves stacked high with pornography
and fishing loors, I hear the belch of an engine.
It's a big black car. pulling in. like a limousine.
blacked-out windows and a chrome bumper,
there may or may not have been blood and

entrails smeared across the front of it but either way, and this guy is stepping out of the car one leather boot at a time and as the first one hits the ground i swear i heard a distant guitar play A minor and i pictured a cut-away shot of a bird cawwing high above us. but either way the light is glinting off the black of this hulking man's outfit – he's square in places you and i are round and he's long in places we could only dream of and it's one of those american days that's so hot the sun is sweating and this guy? wearing all black, cool as a motherfucker. not that fucking your own mother is really all that cool. but this guy? was cool. looked like an assassin when i first looked at him but i blinked and realised he was a priest. I mean he was still tall, still built like an assassin, but the black clothing? That was his gown thing and he even had that little white square on his collar, his dog collar but not like in the military, and not only does the car have a chrome bumper it has a chrome jesus medallion to match – a chrome crucifix where the chrysler emblem should be – and i think gosh this is a priest with a budget. either way i turn and enter the little store, the little gas station hut and there behind the counter is a blind kid – 6 or 7 years old, cute as one of those spare buttons they sew onto the bottom of new shirts.

i hear a high-pitched gasp from outside and it can only be her gasp, so, i peer out that little window by the cash register and i see that the man, the priest, the assassin is washing the windshield of our not-quite-a-cadillac with one of those squeegy stick things and i can see her beehive wiggling frantically as she tells him it's not necessary and please just move along.

sensing something dangerous is about to
happen, or perhaps willing something dangerous
to happen, i remove the ipod from my pocket
and i say to the kid behind the counter 'hey kid,
ya ever sat down and really listened to ziggy
stardust?'

'why no, i don't suppose i have' the blind kid
said.

'it's a seminal album, you're gonna love it' i said
as i placed my headphones over his ears.

as i exited the little hut i was feeling pretty proud
of my quick thinking but a little dirty having
just said the word seminal to a 6 year old. in fact
you should probably never reference ejaculate
in front of someone who within your living
memory…was ejaculate.

(that seems like a logical guideline
for maintaining a healthy form of
compartmentalisation.)

so, i'm out by the car by now and the two of
them are wrestling this squeegie thing, this
window cleaning stick, back and forth out of
eachothers hands like a silent comedy skit.
'listen here laurel and hard-on' i said i said 'i

don't know what gives but you'd better knock it
off or i'll have to break it up, you understand?'

when just at that moment we locked eyes,
he and me, this priest and me, and i swear it
was like looking into my own eyes. the whole
structure of his face seemed to break and reform
under the skin to resemble mine – where he had
been bald before he now had the beginnings of a
pretty nifty hair-do.

'hey man, what the actual fuck?' i asked
articulately and the man, slowly stealing my
face, wrestling a gas station implement out of
the hands of my sort-of girlfriend said 'i've been
following you two sinners for three days – i don't
like your driving, i don't like your premarital
sex and i don't like your incessant references to
music i have never heard of. i am gonna clean
your filthy car and then i am going to clean your
filthy souls and if at the end of it all you would
like to make a donation to the church the lord
will thank you kindly'.

'no way buster. we like our souls dirty and we
like having to drive this car with our heads
hanging out the window cause the windshield is
too dirty to see through.'

'and we will not be making a donation' she said.

'this trip is very tightly budgeted – my nazi
father didn't leave me nearly enough money to
start throwing it in your theological toilet bowl'

'yeah' i said 'and i think i speak for the both of
us when i say that our pre-marital sex is okay too
and even if it's not, that's between me and her
and our respective psychiatrists and is absolutely
none of your fucking business.'

the priest, the assassin,

had now nearly completed his transformation
and was looking exactly. like. me.

'you two are sinners' he said 'and at least one of
you is foreign. now i can't fix the foreign part but
you're on my turf and i can sure as hell try…'

'let me stop you there' she said

'because right about now i'm finding it pretty
hard to tell which one of the two of you is which.
and whichever one of you is the real chris is
gonna know just how turned on i get during
arguments…'

she winked at me.

'stop this' he says as she approaches and starts
running her hands up and down him

'i can't do this' as she wiggles her beehive all up
in his face

'i don't know what kind of crazy games you…'

and just then?

she started urinating on him –

which is something we'd only ever joked about
doing (to one another [urinating on one another
{urinating on to one another}]) but watching it
happen in this moment i wondered if that, like
so many jokes, was coiled around something we
were sorta serious about.

now.

this is the part where things might have got a
little out of hand.

if we'd turned back now – with having teased
and humiliated him a little and forced just a
smidgen of our heathen lifestyle onto him then
i think we mighta been on the right side of the
moral line.

but we didn't stop there.

oh no.

so, she's straddling him and urinating and i
think 'well this is a coming of age story no
longer', here we are having a threesome with a
priest who may or may not be an assassin in a
deserted gas station while a blind kid listens to
david bowie on my ipod just metres away. and
it's only then, with thinking the word threesome
that i realise that i am in a threesome so not
wanting to be left out i run round the side of
the car and i start massaging his head – you

know, start gentle, cause ya gotta give yourself
somewhere to go, so i'm massaging his head and
she's shaking her beehive allover the place and
i'm massaging his head and i look over at the
jesus medallion on the front of the big black car
and i swear to god the jesus medallion, the little
crucifix, winks and licks his little chrome lips
like a porno movie director. so i'm massaging
this guy's head and he's trying to pull away so
i tighten my grip and doesn't the fucking thing
come off in my hands! doesn't his fucking head
come off in my hands and i'm thinking 'what
the hell am i gonna do now?' so i do the only
natural thing i can think of and i chuck the thing.
i throw the thing way up into the air. the head,
from dog collar to hair-do is twirling through
the air, pissing brains out of its neck hole all the
way, and as i am watching the head make its
skyward trajectory i am distracted by motion
in my peripheral vision so i turn and i spot the
jesus medallion on the front of the car. the little
jesus is furiously masturbating and gasping as he
watches this scene. ejaculate arcs through one
of his hand holes like a mucus poodle jumping
hoops at the world's smallest dog show and
Klang as the priest's head ricochets off one of
the gas pumps and i kid you not it lands neck
down and is impaled on a nearby cactus.

the sun is still glaring.

the headless cadaver has had its top whipped off
like a bottle of beer and is now frothing innards
like heineken all over the desert floor. my almost

girlfriend is adjusting her beehive and has a look
all over her awesome little face that says 'we sure
are in the thick of an adventure now, friend!'

i listen out for another A minor chord or
perhaps an E7 but all i can hear is the sound
of our breath – a-rhythmic from excitement,
playing counterpoint with the whistling of wind
and i listen really carefully and hear the sound of
'suffragette city' playing tinny in earphones just
metres away.

she looked at me.

i looked at her.

and we both agreed it was probably time we left.

('wowee mr. you were right – this album is real
good!' the kid says as he hands me back my
ipod and points us in the direction of our hotel.
'but what does the word seminal mean? you said
the music was seminal…what's that?'

[oh jeez.] 'well kid, seminal. seminal means…it
kinda means the journalist is being a bit of a…it
basically means like, really good.'

the kid stares all adorable like and I kid you not
the kid says 'well I sure hope you folks come
back and ask for directions again soon…it's been
seminal to meet you!')

i turn to approach the car, and i notice in my
peripheral vision the little chrome jesus who is
now red in his little chrome face and he says
'uhhh, excuse me mr – you aren't gonna tell my
dad, are ya?'

and i go 'no no jc. you are alright with me.'

we got in the car.

we got in the car and we drove.

we drove and drove, deeper into the desert.

rolling down the curve of the dustbowl on
wheels like rubber milk.

we drove

the wind licked us rough like a cat's tongue

we drove

and i thought about the word cat –

both its jazz-band and whorehouse connotations
and i thought about the word pussy too

about its triple connotations –

vagina, kitty cat, cowardice.

and i reckoned the vagina to be one of the
bravest human organs – accepting of

strangers, not exactly queasy about blood – and
i made a pact with myself to never use

that word to illustrate cowardice ever ever ever
again.

and i thought about the word asshole too –

the desert became dirt became gravel, became
an endless strip of motels.

and we drove

the desert became dirt became gravel, became
an endless strip

we cut a new vein across america

watched over by the sky or by god or maybe just
satellites

we drove

a starless dome up above us

she chain smoked and i contemplated america

out the window

i contemplated its myriad connotations...

...

bullet blast, bullet blast

as the gun kissed you dead

free at last, free at last,

as the zee devoured the zed,

and it bled, and it bled,

the blue the white

and it bled

we are dying, we are dying, we are dead, smart
ass said,

melted into air and powder smoke,

under satellite and sedation, she drove,

these words they leave my lips and explode like
bricks like bricks like bricks,

mean nothing, mean air, mean i had an impulse,
i had nature, i had the evolutionary toolkit to be
able to form this sentence and the humility to
know that it means nothing.

and the muzzle said and the muzzle said as it
branded sulphur moons to the side of your head,

and saltpeter licked his wounds, and oxygen said
'i am an animal placed here by god to be hunted
by you'

and the asshole was dead decades before they
rigged the vote

before the bullet blazed subsonic trails across his
gently swallowing throat

'i thought it'd feel better' i said, (lubricated by
the moist paste of disappointment)

'i thought it'd feel better' i said 'killing a man i
have so often wished dead.'

and with our savage tongues we lick the wounds
of our loved ones

an unconventional weapon of pyrotechnic
composition,

a blade in the mouth all coated in food,

this tongue

is no longer an instrument of taste

or a sticky rope for coaxing nourishment in
through the face,

nor is it a hot-breathed fuck tool unafraid of your
germs.

for tonight it is a weapon

for tonight it is a whip

and with our savage tongues we spray our
enemies' blood all up these fucking walls.

and with our savage tongues we reclaim the
future

and pronounce this language dead,

we carve the map in greased saliva, demanding
enemies' heads,

and the only blurred line is an enemy,

and they suck sulphur moons from metal
cylinders and and and and and and and and

and and

there is no great conspiracy.

your life is not a thriller.

nobody's head is going to come off in your hands.

your fear is normal it is a product of the times
we are living in. it's a disease and a lot of people
have it. it does not make you special. whether
it's Y2K or the mayan calendar, whether you're

an environmentalist or a jehova's witness-ist.
it's the same disease. a compulsion, a fixation
on death and the end of days and the arrogant
belief that one member of one species has any
agency in the outcome of the ecosystem.

it's a lack of imagination. we cannot picture
the future because we cannot imagine living
through, surviving, the present. the past; we
know what that looks like. it looks like sepia
photographs and telephones you had to do this
with *(mime rotary phone)*. it looks like martin
luther king and john lennon and emily pancake
throwing herself under a horse. it paved the way
for where we are now and our lives are bathed
in its echo. nostalgia is comforting, nostalgia,
retro, old school is comforting. it's a way to dig
your heels in and slow the acceleration. we are
still processing the past. still dealing with it. but
the future? the future is a car crash or an orgasm.
we live everyday with a sense of acceleration.
everyday more and more technology, more
and more communication, more and more
information as the world shrinks to the size of
an iphone…and you can wrap your iphone
in a rubber cassette tape just to help ease the
transition!

you can hold the entirety of documented human
experience in the palm of your fucking hand. or
at least that's how it's been designed to feel. and
this escalation, this acceleration, each day faster
and faster, faster than the last, feels like a car
revving at top speed, an engine barely contained
by its chassis, like an orgasm is coming or a car
wreck or some kind of release, and we can't
conceive of the engine going any faster because
we're already digging our nails into the armrest

and bracing ourselves into the curves. so in
our minds we hold this picture, this car crash.
this automobile sailing off the road and into a
ravine, b'boom, the orgasm happening. – our
species is so transfixed and salivating over its
own finale, so convinced that its own orgasm is
just around the corner, that it's about to finish its
lovemaking with this ecosystem, and perhaps on
this occasion doesn't feel as though it's done a
particularly good job.

certainly hasn't earned the cigarette.

...

rest assured if this bulge does turn out to be a
revolver it will not be you who gets the bullet.

cause i got a shaky hand and only six chances to
get that fucker right.

...

but the point is: maybe this car does go faster.

maybe there's miles and miles of open road
ahead of us;

maybe our species and our planet are in their
infancy and you just gotta stop digging your
nails into the armrest.

the crowd was cheering, a shot rang out across
the auditorium and it was my time to go
on. hhhh went the crowd as the body of my
predecessor was scraped up off the stage and
i stare at myself in a dressing room mirror,
moments before this performance, framed by a
row of circular light bulbs. beehive is fingering
salami off the deli tray and into her mouth,
chewing with her wide mouth idiot open – not
like a child but like an adult who is past the
point of caring – too nervous for grace, and i'm
hanging onto my hunger, cause for this gamble
i've gotta be as hungry as possible. door swings
open and the circus midget waves us forward,
he's got one of those headsets and a bowtie, spits
in his hand and smooths his hair down. 'bonjour
senor' he says and i feel a breeze coming in from
behind him, coming in from the amphitheatre,
and my skin which is bare, bare naked has been
powdered for consistency of tone and greased
in the name of charisma. beehive joins me,
licking prosciutto oil from her fingers, revolver
in the other hand, and leans her warmth into
me, resting her head on my skinny bare chest,
oiled for combat. embrace slows my pulse a
little, keeps the breeze at bay, insulated by her
warmth. 'ready pooch?' she whispers as she
tugs on my metal chain, my rubber dog collar,
the noose which is all i wear. she says 'ready
pooch?' and she gives me an almost human stare
that says 'don't worry lover, you're gonna live
through this and die of something else.'

'yeah' i say 'i'm ready' when i mean the exact
opposite and i know that she knows that and
we're passing through the bowels of the building
now, blinking lights and cold concrete warmed
by electric cables, we ascend a metal staircase
and the midget leads us out onto the stage and
whispers 'please don't call me a little person,
i actually prefer midget' as he pushes me out
in front of this crowd. whoops and cheers and
trumpets blare. a drum roll. builds tension. like
machine guns. like tension. and a thousand eyes
stare back, hungry for spectacle, for savagery,
for blood. and your blistered sockets glare back
at me, and your mouth it houses your tongue.
for tonight is a weapon, for tonight it is a whip.
the compere glides across the stage, magnificent
and elastic. explains the rules of the game.
MoneyBowl – dead or alive – and she and me
are fighting to survive. a dish is placed in front
of me, empty dogbowl on the stage. and you are
coaxed up out of your seat and from your hands
you drop your wage. and i am forced to eat it –
MoneyBowl – swallowing coins and credit cards,
notes, bills and billfolds whole. your bank details
and pin pass codes, online sales – sometimes
pittance, sometimes loads. i swallow and i gag,
veins scream and stomach's bloated. some joker
puts down peanuts. actual fucking peanuts. and
the compere croons. and 1000s are lined up to
make donations at my altar, and she's behind me
pistol cocked with instructions should i falter. hell
is a game, son. society is an organism, it sheds
what it does not need. you're on trial tonight,
they are praying, paying, baying to watch you
bleed. and in this moment i start to consider the
word 'baying' and whether it could ever be used
to describe to describe something other than a

crowd and in this pause i stop swallowing and
in this pause and i know i've over-thought things
and i know i've over-thought and i can feel the tide
reversing, i can feel the 'come on' she pleads, as
hope bleeds from eyes in the form of tears, and i
think about salt and i think about peanuts and the
sick amongst you leers. 'come on' she pleads, salt
stains her face with tears, but the money is on the
way back up. the money is on the way back. our
freedom scrapes my stomach lining as i wretch and
wretch and wretch. and the crack of the whip of
the compere – for tonight it is a weapon – and the
neurological effects of – she jumps and cocks the
pistol, covers her face with the other hand. and her
beehive looks good in these glinting lights which
are not the sun and in that moment, a sulphur
moon branding the back of my head, i think about
the word/ *(inhale loud and long)*

...

tonight the tongue's a weapon

tonight it is a whip

and with our savage tongues we spray the blood
of enemies all up these fucking walls

and with our savage tongues we reclaim the future

and we stare into eachother, you and i,

holding eachother,

and we apologize

we apologize

for this arrogant hex of a species that we are
ashamed to be a part of

and we are humble, you and i,

we are humble,

pigeon toed and

wide eyed

we are naked and afraid

and we hold eachother

at the base of infinite everything in all directions.

everywhere you look –

a universe of undeniable complexity,

debatable beauty

and meaningless pain.

new ideas being born,

old ones dying.

and with our savage tongues

we lick our loved ones until they are clean

we spray our enemies' blood up these walls

and we pronounce this language dead.

thank you for reading *THIS IS HOW WE DIE*

here's a few blank pages to cleanse yr palate…

and now it's time for *B-Sides and Rarities*

THIS IS HOW WE DIE: B-Sides and Rarities

is

a standalone monologue made from alternate scenes, off-cuts and 'b-material'
and an expanded and re-imagined rendition of the 2nd half of the main show.

the selection of material and exact running order changes performance to performance but the version presented here is the one most frequently (and recently) performed.

track listing...

GAS STATION (alternate take)
DESERT DRIVE (first date version)
ANTI-NATALIST
MIND WHISKEYS
MOTEL
GIBBERISH DINER (WELCOME TO CROTCH ROT USA)
HEAVEN IS AN OFFICE BLOCK
MONEY BOWL (alternate take)
OUTRO

THIS IS HOW WE DIE: B-Sides and Rarities was first developed for Forest Fringe at Latitude Festival 2014 and has since played Abrons Arts Centre in New York City, Shoreditch Town Hall, CPT, Hackney Showroom and the occasional 'house show' in somebody's living room. if you'd like to book a show get in touch... c t bailey@hotmail.com it'd be my honour!

we killed a guy once.

on the the assumption that it was him or us.

retrospectively i'm not so sure it was him or us.

in fact, it's the one thing i feel bad about in all of this.

you see our great big american road trip was going so far so good.

...a little too good maybe.

ya know, like if you're 15 minutes into a movie and nothing exciting has happened yet?

you're faced with two possibilities:

1. danger and intrigue are merely moments away

or 2. you've bought a ticket for a shitty movie.

we'd spent the bulk of her inheritance on this trip and we'd promised ourselves a goddamn adventure...

picture a gas station. one of those old timey,
broken down, two fuel pump gas stations. and
we're in a desert or the dustbowl or whatever
– what matters is that it's flat and there's flies
landing on things you wish they wouldn't land
on. we've pulled into this gas station in our
rental car – not quite a cadillac but you can
picture a cadillac if that helps you. now, she's
driving cause i don't have a license, and she's
looking good. it ain't all about looks but she
is looking real good – beehive hairdo, retro
glasses, the whole routine – and we're pulling
into this gas station to ask for directions, which
to me seems ludicrous cause as far as i can tell
there's only one long, straight road across this
whole fuckin' state. so i get outta the car and i
go into the little hut, the little beat up gas station
shack. and just as i'm darkening the door of this
fine establishment with it's broken wind chimes
and it's shelves stacked high with porno mags
and fishing tackle, I hear from behing me... the
belch of an engine. it's a big black car pulling
in. like a limousine. blacked out windows and
a chrome bumper, there may or may not have
blood and human entrails smeared across the
front of it but either way, this guy is stepping
out of the car one leather boot at a time and
as the first one hits the sand i swear i heard a
distant guitar strumming A minor and i pictured
a cut-away shot of a bird cawwing high above
us. but either way the light is glinting off the
black of this hulking man's outfit – he's square
in places you and i are round and he's long in
places we could only ever dream of. and it's
one of those american days that's so hot the

sun is sweating. and this guy? wearing all black, cool as a motherfucker. not that fucking your own mother is really all that cool. but this guy? super cool. looked like an assassin when i first looked at him. but i blinked and realised he was no assassin. he was a priest. i mean he was tall, built like an assassin, but the black clothing? that was his gown thingy. even had that little white square on his collar, his dog collar but not like in the military, and not only does his big black car have a chrome bumper it has a chrome jesus medallion to match – a chrome crucifix where the chrysler emblem should be – and i think 'gosh this is a priest with a budget'. either way i turn and enter the little store, the little gas station hut and there behind the counter is a blind kid – 6 or 7 years old, cute as one of those spare buttons they sew onto the bottom of new shirts.

i hear a high pitched gasp from outside and it can only be her gasp, so, i peer out that little window by the cash register and i see that the man, the priest, the assassin is washing the windshield of our not quite a cadillac with one of those squeegy stick things and i can see her beehive wiggling frantically as she tells him it's not necessary and please just move along.

sensing something dangerous is about to happen, or perhaps willing something dangerous to happen, i remove the ipod from my pocket and i say to the kid behind the counter 'hey kid, ya ever sat down and really listened to ziggy stardust?'

'why no, i don't suppose i have' the blind kid
said.

'it's a seminal album, you're gonna love it' i said
as i placed my headphones over his ears.

as i exited the little hut i was feeling pretty proud
of my quick thinking but a little dirty having
just said the word seminal to a 6 year old. in fact
you should probably never reference ejaculate
in front of someone who within your living
memory...was ejaculate.

so, i'm out by the car by now and the two of
them are wrestling this squeegie thing, this
window cleaning stick, back and forth out of
eachothers hands like a silent comedy skit.
'listen here laurel and hard-on' i said i said 'i
don't know what gives but you'd better knock it
off or i'll have to break it up, you understand?'

when just at that precise moment: we locked
eyes, he and me, this priest and me, and i swear
it was like looking into my own eyes. the whole
structure of his face seemed to break and reform
under the skin to resemble mine – where he had
been bald before he now had the beginnings of a
pretty nifty hair-do.

'hey man, what the actual fuck?' i asked
articulately and the man, slowly stealing my
face, wrestling a gas station implement out of
the hands of my sort-of girlfriend said 'i've been
following you two sinners for three days – i don't
like your driving, i don't like your premarital
sex and i don't like your incessant references to
music i have never heard of. i am gonna clean
your filthy car and then i am going to clean your
filthy souls and if at the end of it all you would
like to make a donation to the church the lord
will thank you kindly'.

'no way buster. we like our souls dirty and we
like having to drive this car with our heads
hanging out the window cause the windshield is
too dirty to see through.'

'and we will not be making a donation' she said.

'this trip is very tightly budgeted – my nazi
father didn't leave me nearly enough money to
start throwing it in your theological toilet bowl'

'yeah' i said 'and i think i speak for the both of
us when i say that our pre-marital sex is okay too
and even if it's not, that's between me and her
and our respective psychiatrists and is absolutely
none of your fucking beezwax.'

the priest, the assassin had now nearly
completed his transformation and was looking.

exactly. like. me.

'you two are sinners' he said 'and at least one
of you is foreign. now i can't fix the foreign part
but you're on my turf and i can sure as hell try...'

'let me stop you there' she said

'because right about now i'm finding it pretty
hard to tell which one of the two of you is which.
and whichever one of you is the real chris is
gonna know just how turned on i get during
arguments...'

she winked at me

'stop this' he said as she approaches and starts
running her hands up and down him

'i can't do this' as she wiggles her beehive all up
in his face

'i don't what kind crazy games you...'

and just then?

she started urinating on him –

now.

this is the part where things might have got a
little out of hand.

if we'd turned back now – having teased and
humiliated him a little. having forced just a
smidgen of our heathen lifestyle onto him then
i think we mighta been on the right side of the
moral line.

but we didn't stop there.

oh no.

so, she's straddling him and urinating, spraying
a white-yellow gush allover his chin, and i'm
thinking 'well this is a coming of age story no
longer', here we are having a threesome with
a piss stained priest who may or may not be
an assassin in a deserted gas station while a
blind kid listens to david bowie on my ipod just
metres away. and it's only then, with thinking
the word threesome that i realise that i am in
a threesome so not wanting to be left out i run

round the side of the car and i start massaging
his head – you know, start gentle, cause you
gotta give yourself somewhere to go, so i'm
massaging his head and she's shaking her
beehive allover the place and i'm massaging his
head and i look over at the jesus medallion on
the front of the big black car and i swear to god
the jesus medallion, the little crucifix, winks and
licks his little chrome lips like a porno movie
director. so i'm massaging this guy's head and
he's trying to pull away so i tighten my grip and
doesn't the fucking thing come off in my hands!
doesn't his fucking head come off in my hands
and i'm thinking 'what the hell am i gonna do
now?' so i do the only natural thing i can think
of and i chuck the thing. i throw the thing way
up into the air. the head, from dog collar to
hair-do is twirling through the air, leaking brains
out of its neck hole the entire way, and as i am
watching the head make its skyward trajectory
i am distracted by motion in my peripheral
vision so i turn and i spot the jesus medallion
on the front of the car. the little jesus is furiously
masturbating and gasping as he watches this
scene. ejaculate arcs through one of his hand
holes like a mucus poodle jumping hoops at
the world's smallest dog show and Klang as the
priest's head ricochets off one of the gas pumps,
and i kid you not it lands neck down and is
impaled ontop of a nearby cactus.

there is a distant rumble like a nuclear blast
or perhaps just somebody else's idea of good
music.

the sun is still glaring.

the rumble shakes the desert soft.

i had the gas pump in one hand and i kid you
i furrowed it into the priest's rectum and i
pumped the fucking trigger. and as my baby fat
fingers were branded by the trigger's matt finish
my sort of girlfriend slid the sulphur pimple
of a matchstick down the sandpaper side of a
tiny matchbox and tossed it into his anus wide
gaping open. the anal lips snapping shut as i
twirled the gas pump in a parody of dirty harry
that nobody was there to notice, the match lit
the gas in his brick shitting ass. like a 6 ft feather
duster or a popsicle made of ash we shook loose
this human artefact, his earth body scattered to
the wind.

"threesomes are better when it's just the two of
us" she said...lighting her 1000th cigarette of the
weekend.

i listen out for another A minor chord or
perhaps an E7 but all i can hear is the sound
of our breath – a-rhythmic from excitement,
playing counterpoint with the desert drone
and i listen really careful and hear the sound of
'suffragette city' playing tinny in earphones just
metres away.

she looked at me.

i looked at her.

and we both agreed it was probably time we left.

('gee whiz mister you were right' the kid says as he hands me back my ipod and points us in the direction of our hotel 'this album is real good! but what does the word seminal mean? you said this music was seminal...what is that?'

'ahh jeez kid...it just means...it means....sorta means the journalist is being a bit...it means good basically. seminal means good.'

'well i sure hope you guys come back n ask for directions again soon...it's been seminal to meet you!'

'yeah, we'll see you soon' i said... forgetting the blind kid was a blind kid.)

we drove and drove, deeper into the desert. rolling down the curve of the dustbowl on wheels like rubber milk. the wind licked us rough like a cat's tongue and i thought about the word cat – both its jazz-band and whorehouse connotations and i thought about the word pussy too and about its triple connotations – vagina, kitty cat, cowardice. and i reckoned the vagina to be one of the bravest human organs and made a pact with myself to never use that word to illustrate cowardice ever ever ever again. and

i thought about our first date – cowardice had
brought that particular episode to mind. and as
the car's wheels spun silent through the desert,
fast on the open road, watched over by the sky
or by god or maybe just satellites and as she
shifted from 4th to 5th and chain-smoked her
1000 and 1th cigarette i surfed on a brainwave
back to our first date. an italian restaurant. you
know the type. sinatra on the jukebox, parmesan
shakers and laminated tablecloths. the waitresses
look like jon bon jovi and smell like his tour bus.
they're clearing the bread baskets and making
room for the main course and i can tell the date
is already going well. we are clicking. but i was
nervous, you know, i was sweating in places
i didn't even know i had sweat glands. and i
thought: why waste my time, i know what i'm
looking for. so i did it, i popped the question,
right there on the first date, shamelessly popped
the question in front of a restaurant full of
strangers, i looked her in the eye and i attempted
a roguish facial expression and i did it, i popped
the question, i said: you don't have a concrete
belief system, do you?

and then i waited.

i waited on a knife's edge for what seemed like
an eternity,

she had no facial expression, it was like she
herself was waiting to receive the answer, it was
like deep inside her brain there was an amateur
dramatics society re-staging 12 angry men,

meanwhile i'm in the restaurant. waiting. on a
knife's edge

eventually she said 'get down off the table, stop
trying to balance on the cutlery; of course i don't
believe in god, and you're an asshole for even
asking.'

and i thought about the word asshole, as the
desert rolled by and our rental car cut a new
vein across america, i thought about the word
ass-hole. the sun was gone now, the sky was
empty, a starless schizoid dome above us, i
thought about the word ass-hole, contemplating
its connotations – a jerk or a mean person. and
i thought about my own asshole... doing a dirty
job that no other body part would want to do,
but a necessary one none the less, and not doing
it in a mean-spirited fashion. if anything my
asshole is humble and dutiful. reliable. certainly
punctual. and i vowed in that moment to never
use the word asshole to describe a mean or nasty
person ever again.

the desert became dirt became gravel, became
an endless strip of motels.

watched over by the sky or by god or maybe just
satellites

we drove

a starless dome above us

empty desert scorched earth rolling by

she chain smoked and i contemplated america

out the window

sweat rolled off me in the heat, pooling like piss
in puddles at my feet

her shifting that gear stick, gripped like she's
jerking off a stallion

she breathing heavy in tandem with the engine

i think i can see her clitoris bulging in her jeans

...

..

.

bullet blast bullet blast

as the gun kissed you dead

free at last free at last

a sulphur moon to the head

i learned it from a movie

yes i learned it from a movie

no a dream

she said

and it bled and it bled

a movie

and it bled

and it bled

and it bled

as it

spread ever outwards

hungry for more, for journey, for photographs,
for new, for knowledge – not that i know
anything but i know where i can look it up –
watched over by the sky or by god or maybe just
satellites,

we are dying, we are dying, we are dead, smart
ass said, somethings are better left un-sediment,
that's what that bone above your ass is all about
– we used to have and have not's that's it, two
kinds of People never believe me when i say i've
got this need, i've got this itch, i never boiled
a bunny man but that don't mean i ain't your
bitch. mean as in ragged tongue nasty… society
is an organism, a species, a bundle of cells, more
in common than we have different, all about
of insomnia is characterized by – please do not
speak about the affliction ruining my life as
though it's got character…

i got a slippery enough grip on reality as it islam
is not a race, it's a religion as rotten as every
apple sauce is like a slang word for booze, refuse
the right to choose, it's a woman's choice and
nine times out of ten it is the right choice. she
got the right to choose so long as she choose the
right choice cuts of fresh meat me outside the
station, i sure am hungr-eed the need to feed to
eat money i'm just saying that whichever ape it
was that originally thought 'i know i'll monetize
the food supply' may have had an evil gene.
that's all folks elvis has left-overs, mountains of
unwanted food… losing a quart of plasma just
listening to you drone on about your upcoming
wedding. if that's what it means to be people
people then you people can count. me. out.side.
as part of the rabble. do you know how many
cctv cameras there are between here and my
lower intestine? let me show you! picture me fair
skinned, fair trade, fair game. a game fair won
is a game fair played, i'm no hippy man; if you
need me i'll be at the nearest starbucks, surfing
child porn on their free wifi and pissing my jeans
while i try and unlock the toilet door with that
fucking customer code on the receipt, my proof
of purchase, my proof that i can afford this, and
that my house is not made of cardboard boxes
piled high in a warehouse, whorehouse, big
house, council house, shared house, my house,
your house, parents house, place, pad, joint ,turf,
domicile, home sweet home away from i love
what you've done with the place home where
the heart is, home not house, hot house, frat
house, cat house, this house, witch house?, that
house, dog house and out house, house proud,
but proud of what exactly? your position in
relation to other people up the street, down the

street, on a different street entirely, or distance
from people who make less money? cause
everybody wants to have the shittiest house on
the nicest street, right? that's the best house to
have. you want cheap rent in a good postcode!
that's like being a pimple on a pornstar's ass…

'eggs-ellent' he smirked in a cartoon parody of
a movie you never saw but you feel a little bit
like you did. it was about to go viral when these
digital brushstrokes, this cultural waste-product,
woke up and realized there wasn't an original
thought in his entire DNA, and you and me link
arms, fleeing this city as it burns to the fucking
ground.

which will no doubt be televised in real time,
broadcast to the sun and projected onto every
flat surface this side of a mastectomy'd chest.
cause the people demand entertainment and the
people deserve to know what's going on and the
people need to know what to spend their money
on – unless they've already spent their money
on a tv license in which case their lithium will
be, minus the occasional indent, uninterrupted.

and he stared up at the sky the cartoonist had
mercifully drawn for him and he stared up at
the sky and said 'as the wheels of evolution
roll forward, lord, please don't count me out'

numbered, surrounded by your enemies, as is
so often the case, can you be sure who has your
back?

cause even our enemies are only ever half
wrong.

you and i,

back to back,

blowing kisses, holding hands,

surrounded by enemies as is so often the case.

i got a teargas canister with your name etched
into it

i got a felt tip, long lips,

got renegade tricks and no wave licks

i got ghetto hips

and a private savings account where i'm saving up to get the snip

cause if people-making is what it means to be people, people,

then count me out.

cause this species could sustain itself on the accident babies made from contraception malfunctioning alone.

i carry the heads of my enemies high into the night,

against synthetic backdrops of ever changing light,

because my soul is for sale.

i stole yours with the click of my camera, and it chokes on celluloid n it chokes on oil, cause there's no place in this town to get an analogue picture developed anymore.

society sheds what it does not need.

...

..

.

i've been to the sexual health clinic 2 times. first
time i went for an sti check.

a bump turned up that i was convinced was a
genital wart...

turned out to be... a genital wart.

the second time we were both there. not the
genital wart – that was thankfully long gone,

but she was there. beehive – immaculate.
glasses, the whole bit.

we're discussing our decision – to 'not keep' the
baby,

we're discussing our decision when two
intelligent women come into the surgery.

they appear to be best friends and from what
i can glean one of them had been (raped). and
that's why they're at the clinic.

intelligent woman a turns to intelligent woman b
and says 'who would bring a child into a world
like this?'

and she turns to me and says 'gosh i was just
thinking about over-population and how
apartment prices keep going up and up and up."

'these are all three very sobering notions' i said.

and then i began to drift

i drifted into a bar

deep inside my mind,

i stretch out a pore on my forehead until i can
squeeze in under the skin and i break a little
hole in my skull with an ice pick and holding my
breath i swim through grey matter and i arrive
at this bar

and there's sawdust on the floor and smiling
cactuses have been painted up on the walls – it
was a tacky western-themed kinda place, or
maybe it was a mexican restaurant – it doesn't
matter, what matters is that there's a whiskey
waiting for me and i sidle up to the bar, maybe
i don't sidle – maybe i just approach. either
way, i end up at the bar. and i drain my glass, a
number of times, and then i consider – 4 times –
and then i consider patronizing the jukebox but
'honkey tonk woman' is already playing. and i
think 'gosh, how nifty – that's the song i would
have played but somebody else has already
paid for it, i happily would have paid but here
i am listening to it for free' and then i figured
that someone smarter than me would be able to
boil this thought down into a prescient witticism
about capitalism or free markets. but i was so
proud to have just used the word prescient i
decided i'd let myself off from the big concepts.

so i drained my glass the fifth and final time,

and i stumbled back out, moments later, hiking
through short hills of brain tissue, crunching
across a thin plate of bone and strolling barefoot
through the long-grasses of my own haircut,
eventually emerging back out into the clinic.
into the waiting room.

and the whole situation seems a little less
threatening, it has soft, smudgy edges on it now
cause of the mind whiskies i'd been drinking.

'are you sure this is the right thing to do?' she
said.

'are you sure this don't make us bad people?'

'i'm not sure' i said 'but i certainly hope it don't'

and as i said that, as i said hope, that p, that
plosive,

that p,

she scrunched up her nose as my breath
p-passed beneath her nostrils.

'you've been drinking mind whiskies again'

she said 'i can smell them.'

uh, no… i haven't…

and she knew that he was a liar,

that his pants were literally…On Fire.

behind the motel reception desk there sat a
human artefact – a sixteen-hundred ounce Hello
Machine.

wasn't the kid from the gas station but it might
as well've been

'cancer is a contract killer' he said 'shot my
daddy dead with one-hundred-thousand
cigarette shaped bullets'

'we'll see about that' she said

as sixty-five-hundred miles away the chain
smoking mouse now lay dead

'it's a non smoking room' he said he said

'cause it's century 21, even here, in the wild'

the human artefact exhaled and the two of us
could smell his lunch

'check out's at 10 am, assuming you survive the
night'

my stomach shrank and despite being black, she
turned a peculiar shade of white

'if death comes for us you tell him to wait his
fucking turn, cause we got season tickets and
front row seats for watching the world burn'

i slid currency across the desk and it was wet
from where i got it

history is half soil, half flesh and i trust no fuck
who taught it

got us to where we are now but

history is not a straight line,

this bulge is not a revolver and how can i love
you (back) when you keep sayin' that everythin's
gonna be fine.

under satellites and sedation we sleep and we
rest and occasionally you and i, we dream,
surrounded by enemies, i have your back.

she sprung a fresh one from the hope chest,
folding dead soldiers down to his filter and i
thought about yellow stained fingers and the
long shadow of the cancer killer.

now she was air tight in the present tense (as you
no doubt know by now);

top drawer eel's hips, a veritable baby vamp, a
surefire safe bet bangtail in it to most certainly
win it,

in other words... she were Popular

now i didn't want to cast a kitten and i'd had a
snootful of coffin varnish already.

but hey – i'm only human.

'cut the alarm clock shit' she said breathing blue
sick out of her skin snorkels and i thought 'if it
was indian hop you know i'd understand...'

'i been hitting on all sixes' she said 'and besides
we ain't insured. who says your contract'll be
renewed tomorrow, skip? you know who's
fueling this death trip? we live for today. cause
it's dead daddies black shirt kale what's kicking
the billy.'

now i didn't wanna flat tire. or be accused of
49-ing. and in a technical sense she was making
sound observations: future tense face stretcher or
not, odds were stacked she'd always get my vote,
and what's a bluenose bunny like me thinking
towards the future for anyhow?

right then i caught a glimpse of a fella with a
bright disease.

we were in a truck stop – booth, window, two
cups of morning, florence at the counter and
fluorescents above her. and outside there's lead
sleds coming and thankfuly going. now this
fella what knows too much came dancing into
my peripherals. and those of you that's of the
drinking disposition, that is adult beverages –
i ain't talkin bout juice boxes or warm milk –
will already know this... when you're steamed
and dixie fried, up to here in growlers and ink...
that the first thing to go is your central vision.
thirsty people talk about blind drunk but it isn't
total blindness that sets in. you get a sort of blind
spot in the middle, but the peripheries remain.
experiencing the world in a sort of... donut
vision.

so this guy knows a little about a lot and he's
flamboyantly enacting a whole rolodex of
bull artist moves for the benefit of the candied
perfume cloud what's standing next to him, that
he no doubt has designs on jungling up with. so
he's purring a thick line of BS into her ear hole
and pressing his orchids into her fundamental
right there up against the breakfast counter
as the good citizens of crotch rot USA are
scorching last night's evils with bottomless cups
of black strap and sun beams make dust clouds
above our seated heads. yeah, this was clearly a
guy who did not respect conventional breakfast
buffet decorum. but for all i knew he had ways
like a mowing machine. and besides, i got a
strong stomach and an open mind. fella looked
like a taxpayer to me.

so i turned back towards beehive, mind my own
beeswax, i took another swallow of mud and re-
engaged with the conversation we were having
– but it seems this exit strategy was a week
overdue and a couple of nickels short.

i felt the kiss of a gun's hard lips

cold and round against my temple,

who knew he was carrying a dogleg so phallic it
dripped seminar

click as he pulled back the hammer –

'you better start using that tongue of yours to say
something that means something

you nonsensical sunburned piece of shit.'

he said.

and believe it or not... he was speaking to me.

'you talk and you talk and you talk and you say nothing.' he said 'if you say one more meaningless word i'll cut out your tongue i'll hollow it out like a fleshy finger puppet and sell it back to you so you can lick your own fuckin balls. you understand?'

and i thought to myself: why do people only ever say 'you understand?' after stuff that's pretty easy to understand.

like, if it's just because they want to sorta underline the point they're making, they could just say it...again. for their own benefit. that'd be more satisfying for them and on the off chance that the other person really-didn't-understand ...then this would actually be a more economic way to achieve the necessary clarification...

so i said: 'no. i don't understand'

and then he goes:

'you pucker, motherfucker.

and i cut off your lips

with a razor blade

careful to get a neat circle

so i can wear your lips as a bracelet.

then i'll snap my fingers

and challenge you to a whistling contest'

and then i said: 'now hang on a minute...that's not... what you said. a minute ago.'

'yeah...? well *this* is...' he said as he cut out my tongue to fashion a finger puppet.

and no. i did not buy it back from him... i have no desire to lick my own Anything.

heaven is an office block

we got into an elevator that took us way up
above the world and into god's office.

a high rise.

it'd been preserved exactly the way he or she
had left it. a desk piled high with papers and
a phone ringing off the hook. but what a view.
what a view from up there, a panoramic view
of ideas being born, whole universes folding
in on each-other. she thought it was a tad 70s
but i kinda liked it. the whole room was kitted
out in teak panelling. television, liquor cabinet,
phone ringing off the hook. walls lined with
photographs, documents, certificates boasting
god's various achievements. this had been a
glorious tenure, a magnificent reign and the
walls were keen that we did not forget it. phone
ringing off the hook so i answered it. i picked it
up, i put my ear to the receiver and i listened

and she was flapping her wings all excited,
trying to get my attention from the other side of
the room, waving this video cassette around but
of course i can't hear her cause i'm listening to
god's telephone:

leaked across this city, snaked and serrated,
broken unhinged, a prepubescent monster naked
and afraid, mother naked and afraid, brother
naked and afraid and this bulge is 'did you
fuckin see that man? did you fuckin see that?'

and she held out a video cassette tape. it had
come out of brown paper packaging she'd found
on the desk. on the top of the in-tray to be
specific. she read out loud from the typed letter
that had come with the videotape. 'to whom it
may concern. we regret to have to inform you
that one of your key servicemen, god, expired
pre-naturally whilst holidaymaking in the united
states of america. deepest sympathies, signed.'
and then a squiggle neither of us could read. she
padded across the room and slid the tape into
the vcr. brown paper packaging in one hand
and remote control in the other, static on the
screen and part of me knew what was coming.
a big part of me. static gave way to grainy black
n white footage. cctv footage. of a gas station.
footage of the desert or the dustbowl. it showed
two cars, two fuel pumps and three very blurry
people. a blurry man laid out on the floor and a
blurry image of a girl squatting over him pissing
blurry piss onto him as a blurry image of me
removes his blurry head and throws it into the
blurry sky.

we were the kids that assassinated god.

the crowd was cheering, a shot rang out across
the auditorium and suddenly? it was my time to
go on. hhhh went the crowd as the body of my
predecessor was scraped up offa this stage. and
i stare at myself in a dressing room mirror, just
moments before this very performance, framed
by a row of those circular light bulbs. beehive
is there… fingering salami off the deli tray and
folding it into her mouth, chewing with her
wide mouth idiot open – not like a child but like
an adult who is past the point of caring – too
nervous for grace. and i'm hanging onto my
hunger, cause for this gamble i've gotta be as
hungry as possible. door swings open and the
circus midget waves us forward, he's got one
of those headsets and bowtie, spits in his hand
and smooths his greasy hair down. 'bonjour
senor' he says and i feel a breeze coming in from
behind him, coming in from the amphitheatre,
and my skin which is bare, bare naked, has been
powdered for consistency of tone and greased in
the name of stage charisma. beehive joins me,
licking prosciutto oil from her fingers, revolver
in the other hand, and leans her warmth into
me, resting her head on my skinny bare chest,
oiled for combat. embrace slows my pulse a
little, keeps the breeze at bay, insulated by her
warmth. 'ready pooch?' she whispers as she tugs
on my metal chain, my rubber dog collar, the
noose which is all i wear. she says 'ready pooch?'
and she gives me an almost human stare that
says 'don't you worry lover, you're gonna live
through this and die of something else.'

'yeah' i say 'i'm ready' when i mean the exact
opposite and i know that she knows that and
we're passing through the bowels of the building

now, blinking lights and cold concrete warmed
by electric cables, we ascend a metal staircase
and the midget leads us out onto the stage and
whispers 'please don't call me a little person,
i actually prefer midget' as he pushes me out
in front of this crowd. whoops and cheers and
trumpets blare. a drum roll. builds tension. like
machine guns. like tension. like a drum roll. and
a thousand eyes stare back, hungry for spectacle,
for savagery, for blood. and you're blistered
sockets glare back at me, and your mouth it
houses your tongue. for tonight it is a weapon,
for tonight it is a whip. the compere glides across
the stage, magnificent and elastic. he explains
the rules of the game. MoneyBowl – dead or
alive – and she and me are there, and we are
fighting to survive. a dish is placed in front of
me, empty dogbowl on the stage. and you are
coaxed out of your seat and from your hands
you drop your wage. and i am forced to eat it –
MoneyBowl – swallowing coins and credit cards,
notes, bills and billfolds whole. your bank details
and pin pass codes, online sales – sometimes
pittance, sometimes loads. i swallow and i gag,
veins screaming and stomach's bloated. some
joker puts down peanuts. literal fucking peanuts.
and the compere croons and 1000s are lined up
to make donations at my altar, and she's behind
me pistol cocked with instructions should i
falter. hell is a game, son. society is an organism,
it sheds what it does not need. you're on trial
tonight, they are praying, paying, baying to
watch you bleed. and in that moment i start to
consider the word 'baying' and whether it could
ever be used to describe to describe something
other than a crowd and in this pause i stop
swallowing and in this pause i stop swallowing

and i know i've over-thought things and i know
i've over-thought – i can feel the tide reversing,
'come on' she pleads, as hope bleeds from eyes
in the form of tears, and i think about salt and
i think about peanuts and the sick amongst
you leers. 'come on' she pleads, salt stains her
face with tears, but the money is on the way
back up. the money is on the way back. our
freedom scrapes my stomach lining as i wretch
and wretch and wretch. and the crack of the
whip of the compere – for tonight it is – and the
neurological effects of – she jumps, she cocks the
pistol, she covers her face with other hand. and
her beehive looks good in these glinting lights –
which are not the sun, no matter how hard we
pretend – and in that moment, a sulphur moon
branding the back of my fucking head, i think
about the word glint/ (inhale loud and long)

this planet spins

sensitive but indifferent

hollow and vainglorious

a callous husk

a snaking boulder rolling across an infinite black
starscape

our planet is indifferent to us

our planet will out survive us

outsource us

and if necessary out-force us

our planet will force us out

cause

our planet is indifferent to us

made from different stuff than us

and we stand

back to back, you and i,

quivering naked

together.

in the face of indifference

in the knowledge that it could be different

and we have got eachothers back

surrounded by enemies

as is so often the case

an enemy approaches...

we blow him a kiss

and when he turns his back

you and i ?

we blow him away.

WWW.OBERONBOOKS.COM

Follow us on www.twitter.com/@oberonbooks
& www.facebook.com/OberonBooksLondon